STREET MUSIC

Poems by Mike Marqusee

To Kat,

In solidarity,

Mike Marqusee

ABOUT THE AUTHOR

Born and raised in the suburbs of New York City, Mike emigrated to Britain in 1971, age 18. Since the late 70s he has lived in and around north London (currently resident in Stoke Newington) and been active in a variety of political and social causes and campaigns, local, national and international. As a member of the Labour Party for nearly twenty years, including a long stint as editor of the left-wing *Labour Briefing*, he was closely involved in the struggle against the (ultimately successful) takeover of the Party by the forces of 'New Labour'. He finally resigned in 2000. Since then he's taken part in anti-war, pro-Palestinian and anti-cuts campaigns, as well as continuing his long-standing engagement with south Asian politics and culture.

His published writing covers a wide and eclectic range of topics, from cricket and music to the politics of identity and mass resistance (and back). In a series of books noted for their originality and readability, he has deftly explored the intersections between politics and culture, always from an unapologetically egalitarian and democratic perspective. He writes regular columns for *Red Pepper* (in Britain) and *The Hindu* (in India). For an archive of his work and details about all his books see www.mikemarqusee.com

Also by Mike Marqusee

If I Am Not for Myself: Journey of an Anti-Zionist Jew (2008)
Wicked Messenger: Bob Dylan and the 1960s (2005)
Redemption Song: Muhammad Ali and the spirit of the sixties (1999, new edition 2005)
War Minus the Shooting: a journey through south Asia during cricket's World Cup (1996)
Anyone But England: an outsider looks at English cricket (1994, new edition 2005)
Defeat from the Jaws of Victory (co-author) (1992)
Slow Turn, a novel (1986)

STREET MUSIC

Poems by Mike Marqusee

clissold**books**

First published by Clissold Books 2012

ISBN 978 - 0 - 9572088 - 0 - 3

Designed by Audiografix
Cover art by Zoran Jevtic
Printed and bound in Great Britain by
CPI Group (UK) Ltd, Croydon, CR0 4YY

Copies of this book can be obtained from
www.mikemarqusee.com

clissold**books**

CONTENTS

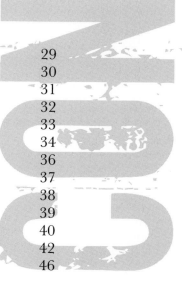

III *Thriving in the dark*

IV *The Book of Liz*

V *The diamond's role*

POETRY AND PROSE (BY WAY OF AN INTRODUCTION)

Poetry was an early discovery and has remained a constant if sometimes shadowy companion, even during those times (years) when I was consumed with the priorities of the political moment, with the determinedly prosaic. Poetry was an escape, an indulgence, but also a guide, a provider of meaning.

At university in the early '70s I gobbled up the canon of English poetry (as then constructed) with a wide-eyed, visceral delight. At the same time I had my first experience of love, with all the usual ups and downs, and like so many others in similar circumstances took to writing poetry. For a couple of years I applied myself to it. And I was serious about the craft. Then I gave up. Partly because I became absorbed in work and politics. But mainly because I had no confidence in myself as a poet (or indeed much else). What did I have to say? What meaning could be distilled from my narrow experience? What style (whose style) should I adopt when I had no style of my own?

So I set about a long excursus in the domains of prose. In hindsight, my judgement about my own limitations at that time was correct, though it saddens me that for twenty years I barred myself from writing so much as a single line of verse.

Even so, poetry was always there, in the background, providing resonance, illuminating at moments the most mundane tasks. Blake, Shelley, Wallace Stevens, Garcia Lorca, Mahmoud Darwish, the Hebrew prophets, Nazim Hikmet, Kabir, Dylan, Rilke, Ginsberg, Hugh MacDiarmid, Langston Hughes: encounters with these poets (and others) have been way-markers and spirit-shapers. Not influences on my poetry so much as on my life.

My writing has also been grounded in other, less rarefied forms of literary activity. I worked for many years sub-editing other people's prose, often submitted by untrained writers. This was an intimate engagement with language and its disciplines, an artisanal experience from which I learned much and whose lessons I like to think are embedded in both my prose and my poems.

It was writing about that heroic world-shaker and minor versifier Muhammad Ali, and his links to African-American music and literature, that enticed me back into scribbling poetry in the late '90s, after a long hiatus. I applied myself to it with increasing focus over the following decade, despite the distractions of the war on terror, but scarcely stopped to reflect on what this scribbling amounted to, if anything.

I turned back to poetry because I had nowhere else to go. Prose, at least the kind I'd worked hard to master as a journalist and historian, couldn't do the work that needed doing. There was no alternative. Not for me, given my limitations.

These limitations took a new form when in June 2007 I was diagnosed with multiple myeloma, a haematological cancer. One effect of the illness was to spur me to act on the advice of friends and in 2009 I published (in a very limited print run) a selection from the previous decade's worth of poetry.

Street Music brings together poems written in the two years since then (2009-2011). These poems are the product of circumstances not of my choosing, not only my entanglement with illness but other, wider entanglements in a period of turmoil.

Wallace Stevens described 'the poem' as 'the cry of its occasion'. I don't think of these poems as 'cries', but they are all certainly responses to their occasion, or perhaps discoveries of that occasion, attempts to know it to the full. When I was first diagnosed I joked with friends that I was determined not to add to the catalogue of cancer confessionals. But as it turned out the experience of illness, the complex reality of cancer with its multiple points of pressure, did not permit that evasion. The result is *Multiple Myeloma, a suite*, the sequence of poems which comprises the first section of this book and which is meant to be read as a whole. I really couldn't say it any other way.

In journalism or history there's little room for discontinuity, for ellipsis, for far-fetched digressions and zones of silence. Sometimes poetry's indirection is the only route to the heart of the matter.

Mike Marqusee
Stoke Newington, London
January 2012

MULTIPLE MYELOMA, A SUITE

IT WAS THE MAP THAT THREW ME OFF

IT WAS THE MAP THAT THREW ME OFF

I've been trying to measure the phases
since the morning I left the clinic, walked
on the pavement next to loud traffic and everything
seemed calm, specific and no more than itself.

I've been trying to measure the phases.
Treatments, blatant and insidious,
side effects blooming like hot-house orchids,
symptoms within symptoms,
sequences and non-sequiturs. Cross-lapping
waves. Reefs of feeling. Maroonings.

Phases marked by deviations from putative norms,
new uncertainties replacing old,
all merely natural, grey lichen on grey rock.

Phases of more than one moon,
and none is like another: each brings its own ache
or impediment, its own surge of relief.

It was the map that threw me off,
seduced me into thinking there was a right track
while leading me down the wrong one.
The streets it named I could not find,
the streets I found had other names -
or perhaps they were hiding on another map in another city?

Embarrassingly late, I stumbled on the secret.
It's only on maps that north is up and west to the left,
that the shortest distance between two points is a straight line,
that stiff ascents are dissolved into equal and effortless steps.

SIDE EFFECTS

My stomach hovers on the far side of the room,
sulky in rebellion,
while the space it's abandoned
is a vacuum that abhors nature.

The cure's another disease
not better or worse but different:
a confusion of inside and outside.

The stomach is a fickle deity.
It spurns all offerings.
I wonder how I can appease it
just for a moment,
just long enough to lure it back into place.

Negotiations are fraught with mistrust.
The ceasefire is fragile.
My stomach hovers on the far side of the room.

BLOOD TEST BLOOD TEST

In my sample they found today's *Morning Star* headline,
an elevated indignation count,
images of Monument Valley
and a much depleted patience ratio.

They found the excess iron of sadness,
the micro-grit of causes not given up.
They found platelets sleek as tiles,
stem cells like motorcycle gangs,
red and white corpuscles exchanging courtesies
and also those enemies within, renegades by instinct,
dogged survivors, myopic boot-boys,
prolific and all-consuming.

Their search is only for room to live,
their purpose only to grow,
to multiply, to thrive like any living thing.
But the more they thrive
the more their habitat is hollowed out.

In the end they perish with the husk of their host -
a pitiable life cycle,
somewhat like our own.

CRAMP

What's that demon riding my muscle?
What pleasure does it take in plucking that fibre?

Spasm running along the thick knuckle.
Contortion of the buckled finger.
Tendon taut, an over-tuned string.
Hand in lock-down.

Demon, are you malevolent or indifferent?
An agent of revenge (then whose?)
or an imp of irony (but where's the joke?)?

Do you do it just to show it can be done,
just to remind me who's boss?

Like a school yard bully, you pick on me.
Like a false friend, you jab at a sensitive spot.

Or are you just another palpable invisibility
over which we have no control,
whose only demand is our endurance?

TAKING THE WATERS TAKING THE WATERS

These waters may not be curative
but they're therapeutic.
The odour keeps discomfort at bay.
The warmth smooths transitions.
The belch from the earth's offal -
the foetid aerosol -
dispersed in the mineral atmosphere
gives the air density
and the waters a slick silkiness.
I met a patient who swore by them
though with his blotched skin and yellow eyes
he looked half dead already.

FAMILIAR INTRUDER FAMILIAR INTRUDER

The room is in denial.
On the prowl, phone to ear, feet
patterning the floor,
I practise the art of evasion.
I pay little heed to the grinning solemn
sober hungover pallid dark figure
hovering in the doorway,
barely suppressing jackass bray
from lips of madrigal.

****

Mystery guest, introduce yourself.
You walked in from inside
as if you belonged here, as if you were me.

Coming down for breakfast
joining the table with coffee mug
barely disturbing domestic routine...
You've left me no place to hide.

Surely your non-chalance is assumed,
as artificial as my own.

*****

The movies used to like it that way:
quick, clean deaths, gore and suffering veiled.
But the aesthetic has changed;
it's become an anaesthetic.

I prefer the *siguiriya,* where the pain is probed
amid an infinity of micro-tones and a metallic
flourish of the guitar. In a world of bright screens
I prefer the under-illumined, the shadow's elisions,
the suggestion whispered by a face seen in profile.

****

Everywhere, you have your impersonators,
mimicking your deferential manner,
refining your targeted indifference,
lurking in plain sight.

Wearing the history of love that dies,
inch by crippling inch, slouching
alone at a corner table,
crepe skin falling from dull eyes
that do not bother with the menu:

Obscure collaborator, have no fear!
I'm not one to shoot the messenger.

IN THE DAY UNIT

The ash blonde woman with papery face
dozes, head bowed, eyelids heavy with mascara,
while her companion reads in the *Daily Mail*
of the kidnapped yachtsman and the world's hottest curry.
She is only half awake herself.

A nurse whose name is forest-flower in another language,
efficient in wide waisted trousers,
slides the needle under the skin, finds the vein, wounds
with gentle intent and a slow-tender demeanour
that reminds patients of mothers they never had.

We're all hooked up, we're tethered,
our tubular manacles light-weight,
flexible and nearly transparent.
Cannulae in place, drips steady, we find
small dreams hovering in the air
we breathe without assistance.
Air of the day unit, busily calm!

There's nothing coy in the muffled voices
just a search for the meaning of the word 'subdued',
All these life-death matters dealt with as matters-of-fact,
seamlessly stitched into workplace banter,
the codeless code that lubricates the cycles of the day,
the hours of unequal dimensions,
the seconds squeezed out like intravenous drips.

Hush as soothing as the trickle of sweet tea!
Air of the day unit, busily calm!

I FEAR THE SHRINKAGE

I fear the shrinkage.
The narrowing field of vision,
the circumscribed reach,
circumscribed sympathies,
the imprisoning rhythm of discomfort and relief.

I fear the enclosure, the selfishness.
I fear not being stirred by news of foreign revolutions.

I fear having my borders redrawn
moving only between adjacent rooms.
I fear living by the narrow laws of analgesia
with elaborate strategies in pursuit of minimal ends.

I fear the shrinkage, the helplessness,
the loss of faculties, of pleasures,
of a purpose other than managing pain.
I fear becoming a sponge
sufficed to absorb what's given me.
I fear the horizontal perspective.

I fear living from tea cup to tea cup.
I fear the cracks in the tea cups
growing larger than cracks in empires
or ideological rifts.
I fear the shrinkage.

I fear the turning inward.
I fear being reduced to my resentments
with nothing to protect me from my jealousies.
I fear caring only about the texture of the sheets.
From my diaphragm I fear
the all of it, the none of it.

I fear losing myself in the immediacy of the final stages,
the enveloping monochrome, the intrusive close-ups,
the contracting horizon of desire.

REDUCED AND ADRIFT

REDUCED AND ADRIFT

This evening I'm reduced and adrift.
I've lost track of the day, again.
It flies away from me,
like an unchecked checklist.
It flies away from me and I think for once
I'll let it go, wherever it goes.

This evening I've forgotten how to exert myself.
My marrow is watery, my limbs too light
to carry their load, to rise from the sofa
which floats on an ocean.
I can hear sounds from a mainland
but have no idea which direction they come from.

This evening took me by surprise.
Its shoes must have soles of softened leather.
It must have a neat and cautious stride.
It creeps in softly and suddenly I'm surrounded.
It's this wanting not to disturb me
that really disturbs me.

Because this evening,
nothing hangs right. There's no balance
sturdy enough to take a next step.
The telephone rings and keeps ringing.
It's my fault for not answering it.
I've drifted too far out.
I don't want a rescue mission -
I'm not up to it: the floodlights, the intrusion,
the gratitude.

KEEP YOUR ANGER INTACT

No envy for those yet to be born,
slick and sticky, lips puckered for the breast,
headed for the flood-time,
the barter economy, the land slip,
the social crunch.

I know what it's like
being dead before you're dead,
all traces wiped. You look back
and not one footprint is visible.
You got here but god knows how.

I'm not afraid of being nothing
so much as losing something,
so much as leaving someone.

Still I'll die with my anger intact.
I'll die with hatred in my gorge,
holy hatred, bitter salve.

I'll die with my anger -
at the smug, the entitled,
the comfortable in their own skins,
at the gate-keepers standing their fiendish watch -
intact and unassuageable.

Sacred animosity, precondition of love!
Redeemer of life's wastes.
I'm almost ready for that death.

COMFORTING THOUGHTS

When I come across one on the way to the hospital
or when I'm offered one by a friend
my eyes narrow. I screen out the glare.
I'm on my guard.

I can't be sure who first taught me to distrust
comforting thoughts
and whether I should be grateful or not,
but I've clung to the lesson.
I've seen off temptations.

The maxim runs: if a thought is comforting
it's unlikely to be true. When you hear
what you need to hear, when what you hear
offers a second chance, a vindication,
you've entered a danger zone. What lurks
is denial, compromise, the demagoguery of the self.

So by distrusting comforting thoughts
I pre-empt disillusion. It's become a habit.
But recently I've asked myself,
is it one I want to carry to my grave?
Is it a habit I'm capable of breaking?
Just what is it I'm afraid of losing?
Why am I so terrified, so tempted
by this leap in the dark?

ON THE OTHER HAND ON THE OTHER HAND

On the other hand, there's nothing I have to do any more.
I wonder how I ever lived with the pressure.
There's nothing I have to do any more
except what I have to do.
The choices come round daily, like meals,
surprising how many there are, how urgent they seem,
how few make a difference, how easily they're forgotten.

There's nothing I have to do any more.
What's done is not only done
it's greater than anything more that could be done.
The future is only for finishing touches.

There's nothing I have to do any more
except watch John Ford movies, listen to Cameron de la Isla,
gaze at one more sea under the canopy of night,
plan one more itinerary, take one last flight
to a place where I'm close up against the wind,
where the earth is touchable,
where the vast and the ancient lie exposed to intimate view,
where the daily routine is rich with small touches,
like honey on a breakfast plate.

On the other hand, I suddenly find I have prerogatives.
I can select moments, designate priorities.
My excuses are ready-made.
My choices are narrowed to that fine point
where they become infinite.

LATE THERAPY LATE THERAPY

A late therapy, of limited ambitions.
A late therapy, coming after so many others.

A delaying tactic, body-check,
swerve and manoeuvre.

An option to which there is no option.
A not-giving-up, not-giving-in
quite yet therapy.

An affair of containment and deferral.
Eking out a future, costing a fortune.

A late therapy that calls for a late theorem,
a proposition about life
as a dialectic of remission and relapse.

Or is it a too late therapy,
and therefore not really a therapy at all?

ATIVE OF FATIGUE

Insidious toxicity. The drop that poisons the ocean.
The late therapy marks a return to an earlier regime:
nausea and its truncated eruptions,
exhaustion and its metonymies.

I'm tired in the daylight,
which falls around me in cold shafts,
locking me in, locking me away.
I'm tired at nightfall,
and can't take part in its communal bustle.
I'm tired in my sleep,
where every impulse is thwarted,
every movement meets resistance.

It's depressing to think of the object I've become.
There are moments when the subject that I am
rises up against this lowly status.

See that fire reduced to a low glow,
no more than an ember? That's me.
But I'm also that figure at the bellows
trying to rouse a flame.

It's a narrative of fatigue and the hunger for more life.

HOSPITAL VISIT, SPRING

HOSPITAL VISIT SPRING

Today I feel afraid of nothing.
One after another, I've hauled myself over the hurdles.
Now I can idle for a while in a straight stretch.
I've identified those things that will last as long as I will,
on which I can rely: pet hates and the prejudice of love.

Today I'm being examined,
subject to a full spectrum search,
scanned and screened.
I yield up all my secrets.
I release myself to strangers.

Today I'm being cared for
and am content with that.

Today I want to be calm and clear like a philosopher,
to see events in proportion and distil beauty from a stone.

SLEEPLESS 3 AM SLEEPLESS 3 AM

Fickle stomach, fickle senses,
mistaking high pitched odours for their opposite,
mistaking one sense for another.
Sleepless 3 am, under siege. Incomplete –
the days keep wasting themselves.
My eyelids heavy as plush curtains
dragging on the floor
but my mind revving its engine like a teenage boy.

3 am sleepless, dwelling on what's to come,
dwelling on the end times,
my own and everyone else's,
dwelling on what I should be dwelling on
instead of those things I am dwelling on.
No wonder I can't sleep.

Behind the question posed tonight
there hides another question, I'm sure.
And this hidden question may be more pertinent,
more adroit, more worth answering,
though much harder to answer,
than the one that's been keeping me awake.
It may be a question that comes in parts,
as they seem to do these days.

(He's sleeping now, at last.
I don't want to disturb him.
He's been up all night,
pressing pressing pressing
harking and hammering
measuring and plotting,
he's run me ragged.
For god's sake let him sleep now
so I can get some rest.
So I can get a break
from his snarled corrections
and sudden changes of mood.
I need a set of earplugs
that function in reverse,
muffling the ceaseless clamour
emanating from within.)

Technically, I'm asleep
though it feels like something else.
Like choppy seas tossing passengers
against bulwarks. There's no way of knowing
which way you're facing. Like an interview
that turns into an interrogation
when the questioners never let you finish the answers,
and you're not sure you know how to finish them anyway.

Bluffing my way through awkward moments
posing inadvertently pertinent questions,
bluffing my way through finality, hoping to con it
of every available coin...

The temptation is to prepare for it
by wrapping yourself in it, huddling
under a duvet thick with end tidings.
Here at least there's no shiver in the spine.

But if I'm not careful, this thing will crowd me out,
cut me off from the weather.

The doctors' hands are soft, leavening
oncology with sport,
and the occasional retreat to hard science.
Nurses wear their uniforms indifferent to elegance or a neat fit.
This is reassuring...

If I could slough off my ambitions
I could concentrate on this thing.
Get to grips with it, face it off,
not like a boxer in an arena
but like a friend, like the best moments of the best friendships
unfolding through the years in a series of unpublished exchanges.
When you think of it, we are like the stars,
shedding light we don't know where.

From my hospital bed I can see the patch of sky
where the orange glow from the burning prison
flickered on the night of the insurrection.
The rioters passed this way
after torching the Lord Chief Justice's mansion.
They razed the prison to the ground
but left the hospital untouched.

It's as if I've been asked to try out new territory.
Someone has to go ahead. Get a feel
for the unfamiliar environment,
what is and is not important,
what can and cannot be left blank.

It's as if I have to report back from a novel perspective
which is never more than intermittently grasped:
sometimes an elevation, a raising up and over,
with access to a wider view...
sometimes a burial in darkness,
my cramped hands scrabbling at cold dirt...
sometimes a separation, a peeling away,
an equation from which I've been removed.

I'm bluffing it out as best I can
through hailstorms and bee-stings,
past uniformed minsters of all faiths,
past roadblocks and checkpoints
concealing the bomb inside with a calm demeanour -
the bomb whose only victim is the body that carries it.

It's right to feel it coming on.
It sharpens your loves, forces your hand.
It makes decisions count because they're irrevocable.
It makes you realise that all decisions are irrevocable.
Nothing done or undone in an extra twenty years would call them back.
Yet still there's the idea that in the final act the tables can be turned,
the mirror re-angled to bathe the past in a more generous light.

So I'm bluffing it out as best I can.
I've given each rib a name.
The one on the left, third from bottom
I call Jeremiah, a twinge here
prophecies pain to come.

What "else"? I've scrolled to the bottom of the poem
and am none the wiser.

NO NEED FOR UNREST

THE PROPHET IN SECOND CLASS

A man with a stick and a sack
sitting in a second-class railway carriage
explained that his mission was to preach
a total revolution in social relations.
He was a party of one.
He smiled as he declared himself
the last true Communist.

His scarf was dirty, his jaw unshaven,
his teeth scattered.
But what I remember most is the gaiety
in his purple-ringed eyes
as he spoke of the overthrow of the bourgeoisie
and the just, enduring rule of the masses.

THE URBS ON THE HILL URBS ON THE HILL

The urbs on the hill is primitive: a density of angles,
shadow slicing shadow, rooftops
stilled in the dance of unplanned geometry,
denizens safeguarded, except from each other.

It's a compact masterpiece. The sculpture of generations,
carved in bursts, closing
and opening in three dimensions, facilitating wanderings
in a space so small it's easy to get lost
then come back with surprise on your own trail.

Stone, brick, timber, slate, lime, rubble. Everything weighs
on everything else. Outlines softened at edges,
worn by weather and indelicate human touch,
crumbled, crack-laden but still load-bearing, upright,
sky-reaching. Still anchored, monochromatic, modest.

From its patched walls the view is extensive.
The view within more extensive still.
Chambers narrowed, topped, joined,
separated and demarcated. Populated.

The urbs is hushed, blanketed with rumour, full of time.
Anger issues from behind a plastic curtain,
frying smells and radio speech from a kitchen vent.
One after another they follow:
revelations compressed within a compass whose needle
swings wildly, caught between revolution and counter-revolution.

WAYS OF LOOKING AT A DEMONSTRATION

From inside, heads and shoulders,
fragments of banners, the blur
of the slow pace,
the overlapping speech,
the enveloping hubbub,
the communal flow.

From the air, where a periphery
appears and stragglers can be identified.

Look twice, at least. Squint
so your vision is doubled,
so the marchers multiply,
each one matched by a twin, a ghost
standing in for absent company.

Look at it from below, all those purposeful feet
trampling overhead. Arches of the underground
bending with their weight. The bass rumble
of determination and the percussion
of defiance.

Look at it as movement through space and time,
from beginning to end and beyond,
from origins to outcomes and back.

See the demonstration as it is:
its outlines trembling.
See how everyone who joins it
is ever so slightly altered.

Look at it through a spectrometer:
its chemical composition lit up in variant hues,
or use infra-red, measuring the heat of the demo,
or a weather satellite, the cloud of common purpose
looming over London.
Or look at it on TV, with the sound off.

STREET MUSIC STREET MUSIC

Let me tell you about street music.
Busking is a game.
Even the police play along,
depending on your repertoire.

My darbuka man knew how to locate that low,
hollow spot and make it ring like a bell.
But concrete is concrete, you know.
The tiled underground an acoustic black hole.

We looked for natural amphitheatres
and found them on waterfronts and piazzas.
But wherever we sang, we were soon moved on.

I could spot them from a distance,
the passers-by who were going to pass us by
without a glance.
I could see them deafen themselves
and admired the strength of their resolve,
the rigidity of their gaze.
I wrote songs just for them: gentle
melodies, like a light touch on the upper arm.

Dirges were perennial favourites:
melancholy spread like honey
over the ranks of harrowed commuters.
I could sing of losing a lover, a flat, a game of chess -
all that mattered was the loss prefigured in the chord.

Once I was hammering out that line
where Dylan says there's no success like failure
and failure's no success at all,
when a man with a black leather briefcase,
a smooth brow and untroubled eyes
put a twenty pound note in my hat.

Let me tell you about street music.
There's nothing pure about it.
It's a moment by moment compromise.
It's slippery, sarcastic.
It makes a mockery of the WTO.
It takes the piss out of Intellectual Property.
It's recidivist and proud of it.

OBJECT LESSON OBJECT LESSON

What is that crime we keep committing
that we are made so small, so insufficient?
It must be a rare crime, a daily crime,
for us to be kept so low, so discouraged.

Do we commit it in our sleep?
Is it out of a dream?
A shivering jealousy gestating in darkness?
Or is it done in daylight, on TV,
with an insouciance for which we must be made to pay,
for which we must be rendered weak and meagre,
subservient to everything but ourselves?

This purpose only has been assigned us:
to serve as an example,
a lesson in redundancy.

From windows high and wide,
you look down on me and mine,
you calculate our insignificance, subtracting
our illusions from our deficiencies.
Your head swells, superiority
rushes in your blood like crack cocaine.
We below are spared your addiction.
Infinitesimal but free,
inferior and therefore equal.

INDISCRIMINATE

A direct hit on a block of flats
on a cloudless night in the autumn of 1940
buried two hundred people under a pyramid of rubble.

The memorial stone has buckled
but you can still read the names,
German names, Slavic names (Jewish names),
while at the base of the stone
dark-stained leaves pile up in an unmade bed.

When the sirens rang the people with the names
following instructions
crowded into the basement
where there was little air and a smell of sweat.

When the bomb struck the building,
when the building yielded to the bomb,
bodies splintered like violins and cellos.
Under the weight,
even the strings of the double bass snapped
with a loud sound.

Did they hear the music of the bomb screaming
downward in the last seconds before impact?
Before the flats above toppled into each other
interring them in a darkness
of brick, steel, concrete and unbreathable dust?

Their mistake was living on a flightpath,
being at home
when home melted in the spray of imperial fire.

Death out of the sky,
by unmanned drone, helicopter gunship, missile strike
or bombers flying at high altitude
seems arbitrary, indiscriminate.

Indiscriminate, without reference to innocence or guilt,
gender, age, intentions or taste in music.
Indiscriminate, like the public is supposed to be.

In the calculus of Great Powers
the execution of the innocent is a minuscule integer.
The gutted, smoking building, the charred limbs
merely the black flowers of the domination tree.

Children of Hackney:
sweep away those dark-stained leaves,
read the names on the buckled stone,
imagine for a moment
death out of the sky, indiscriminate
but always one-sided.

'ALL IN IT TOGETHER'

The prisoner is not the same as the guard.
The assassin is not the same as the slain witness.
The taker is not the same as the taken.
But their cold embrace
has been declared the totality of social relations.

Great opportunists, Shakespeare knew,
are made by great opportunities.
See now how the future beckons
for the anointed ones: they slough off
the burden of sixty years,
declare their secession
and dream their separate world,
their world of people-like-themselves
clean, clever and invisibly supplied.

Their law is that they deserve
everything they've got and everything
they've not got.
Their ransom notes fill the headlines:
we hold your world in our hands,
pay up or we'll squeeze it like a lemon.
Your only tomorrow
is the one we're prepared to concede.

EGYPT EGYPT

These people filling the square on TV
are our friends and neighbours.
That's not a foreign language they're speaking
though it's an idiom we'll have to relearn.
Let's eavesdrop on their conversations,
see how they name things – freedom, oppression -
see how they tell the difference between names and things.

This is not a dream but like a dream
it's turbulent and calm, long wished for,
full of surprise. As in a dream
time is elided, elongated, hesitant then decisive...
exhausting and renewing. In the square
time is an art-form and space curves with it.

I know this is not a dream because it leaves
definable traces in the atmosphere, like incense.

I know this is not a dream because I have dreamed it before.
I know this is not a dream because like a dream
everything is changed in its wake.

IMPERMISSIBLE ANGER

IMPERMISSIBLE ANGER

We know what your ambiguities conceal.
We hear the undertones; the unstated
slaps us in the face. It leaves a sting,
a red impress, a narrow-eyed memory.

It's just daily life in wisps
evaporating under the journalist's radar.
It's just the sadness of a world of categories
depopulated by decree.

Who ruled this anger impermissible?
Who prescribed these limits?
Why would you stifle someone else's heart?
What would make you do that?

THE TRIBE RENEWS ITSELF

RENEWS ITSELF

Brought to life in the interval between footsteps,
a deviation in the line of march,
the tribe revels in its heyday, its insurgence
prolonged like an opulent meze, dish
after piquant dish, passed around the common table
of an ever-expanding franchise.

There's music, of course,
from the instruments of the tribe.
Strings, percussion and a wide-reeded woodwind
seasoned with the sighs of an artisan
who has shared the tribe's circuitous journey.

In celebration, they overthrow the council of elders.
The ceremony is serio-comic.
The timing flawless.

They break the law down into component parts,
plotting justice on a new periodic table,
debating the configuration
of hitherto unknown elements.

The tribe prises open the moment
like a rusted metal chest,
smashing the lock with a single blow.

Under the cap of night
you can hear the humming
of old questions in new combinations,
amounting almost to collective prayer.

The tribe renews itself with or without excess.
In its box of self-rule are tools we can hardly imagine -
extraordinary optical devices
through which the people come to know themselves.

THE WRECKING CREW

Here they come, the wrecking crew,
the plausible brigands,
down our street in louche pomp.

They come with bailiffs and eviction orders.
They stand outside gossiping
while we number our possessions.
One of them has been delegated
to return our glances with a sigh and a smile.
Maybe he's the worst of the lot.

Last time they reallocated the street numbers.
Now they want us out of the neighbourhood altogether.

When I hear people say it's time
we formed a wrecking crew of our own
I'm almost persuaded.

Here they come, the wrecking crew,
with a train of consultants.
You can tell what they've got in store for us:
a new fangled idea of education in reverse,
an unlearning, a divesting.

They've decided it's time for us to pay their debts.
They've decided the hour is theirs.

Here they come, the wrecking crew,
vandals in fire-resistant uniforms,
shaking blocks of flats like jammed salt cellars,
ferreting out under-5s and planting
inky nightmares in delicate pink brains.

They come at us in waves,
in high frequency bands,
in declining real wages.

There's a fanfare as the crane moves into position
and wild applause as the heavy ball
with its perfect arc
scythes down the troubled estate.

They're systematic,
dismantling structures piece by piece,
adhering to a plan, taking hostages in advance.

We need a gang of bullies of our own,
with our own form of non-negotiable behaviour.
We need to swing the wrecking ball back in their direction,
knock down their mansions and strip their wardrobes bare.
We're only human, which is why
we're in this mess to begin with.
We're only human
and we want to bend our hours to our own cause.

Who'll tire first? Us or them?
We've got to stay focused on the main assault,
find a way to parry the blows,
using their strength as our own.
Who'll surprise whom?
Who'll snare a foot that's taken one step too many?

On their side: the flush of command, the taste for luxury goods,
the natural gas of inflated appetites.
On our side: steadfastness, if we can find it.

SEARCHING FOR AN ASSEMBLY POINT

I was driven into the open by the TV
seeking refuge from its brash blue light.
On the street, under a sagging sky,
I found myself swept along by the atoms
of a crowd searching for an assembly point.

Unemployable, like a man past fifty,
pockets stuffed with post-its,
I pass the cafe that is Joseph's
and the bank that went broke,
I pass Iznik tiles and the dance
of the black cupids on the first floor frieze,
with a song that keeps falling
at the hurdle of the first verse.
If only I could sustain that note -
bottom it out, top it off - I'd find a safer course.

It's a route that never leaves the neighbourhood,
spanning eras and unfinished bridges.
All eyes are fixed on the distance,
apprehensive, as if scanning for a speed trap.
Women dressed for the office wait for a bus,
grinding their teeth at the thought of another
spoilt, absorptive male, empowered
to make them feel redundant.

I observe the formation of triangles,
permutations of betrayal and trust.
Here a battle was won and lost.
Franchises burned through the night.
The peace was disturbed.

A phalanx of schoolgirls marches down the pavement
leaking secrets...
Old friends are spending more time in the pub.
Graffiti can't keep pace with events.
From somewhere there's an angry cry:
 "Wake me up, goddamn it, from this nightmare!"
When I turn to look
the crowd has fissured into a delta
and is passing itself by.

"Whose service do we labour in?
What function are we supposed to serve?"
(I think the voice is mine).
From their eyes I can tell
some have worked late into the night
while others are still half asleep.
Many are being punished solely for being in earnest.

Everywhere I see the impress of hard times,
queues sagging in the middle, reputations
like flags at half-mast.
Conditions of trade are harsh -
it's written on a thousand faces.

The crowd is like all those unanswerable questions:
If a person writes a poem and no one reads it
is she still a poet?
When, where, how do you give up on a friendship?

Yet there's something in them like the colours of the azulejo,
buried deep in the glaze.

In every face I see curiosity insurgent
and curiosity resisted.
It's a fair guess
that all are cultivating at least one secret
and that a few simply aren't capable
of pulling a fast one.

I wonder how much they hear of what's shouted at them?
I like to think it's less than is supposed.
I like to think there's an oversell going on.

Notice how each one carries a childhood,
sometimes on a broad back like a rucksack,
sometimes in the soles of shoes or in a wallet.
As for me, I'm hardly visible these days:
a cane my only mark of distinction.

I'm wondering how a crowd coalesces,
how it finds its assembly point,
how it comes to know itself.
I'm wondering if we can pool our frustrations.
If we can conjure from our impotence
its opposite.

Because
they're taking it apart, piece by piece,
and the pieces are cancelled possibilities,
the pieces are torn from me and mine.
Everything that's in plain sight is hidden.
No benefits, only TV as much as we want,
no universities, only Facebook.

A kind of savage surgery is being carried out,
removing collective memory, leaving us
trapped in the present,
loaded with someone else's debts.

I followed the crowd to the privatised riverfront
where the views are parcelled
and the schoolgates plastered with logos,
where milling children scratching at their labels
whine that this exile is the only life they know.

I followed the crowd in search of an open sea.
At some point we will declare an end
to the measurement of the self against others,
against bright souls from history books,
against characters from fiction,
against the economist's abstraction.
We'll cry out against all measurements,
declare war against inter-measurability itself.
Not one of us is replaceable, whatever they say.

The crowd reminds me that I only put myself
in other people's shoes
because I couldn't find my own
and the common locker was so near at hand.

But why this craving for the blue that splits the grey,
for the fissure in the concrete dome,
for the violence of dawn?
Why this need for shelter, for shadows,
for the comforts of a hot breakfast on a cold morning?
I'm just a snail lost in the herb garden.

When was I ever in command? Enough with that illusion!
If I were a poet, I'd write only of the periphery.
I'd write only of the vengeance of school children.
I'd write that no one was replaceable.

We treasure lost societies for their moments of quiet reflection,
the delicacy of strings plucked by a candle-lit pool,
but I'm still searching for the natural rhythm life's supposed to
have,
where every flood-tide is followed by an ebb,
receding gradually but with a strong song.

The crowd screeches but doesn't halt.
Its mingled breath repudiates commentary.
I understand them all. I'm baffled by them all.
But this is sounder footing. It feels right to keep going
searching for an assembly point.

IT SHOULDN'T BE DIFFICULT

Persuade me: all is for the best
in the best of all possible worlds.
There's no need for unrest.
Persuade me. All I'm waiting for
is a balance sheet, a reckoning.
Persuade me to be content -
it shouldn't be difficult.

THRIVING IN THE DARK

ARRESTED DEVELOPMENT

The child heard someone call his name.
Someone all voice, no body, firm and very near:
it spoke to him as a familiar, with a note of impatience.

It was a voice made famous by repeated long-playings;
and it singled out the child
in the privacy and silence of an attic room, far from parents.

In an attic room, far from friends, safe in a reverie,
the child heard the voice call his name.
(The voice heard in the reverie but coming from outside.)
It called his name and did so, he felt,
with weary purpose. There was no escape.

The child heard the voice call his name
but did not think it in any way unnatural.
He was pleased to be recognised, content
with the calling of his name by that voice,
calling him to a present, implying a future.

In later years, in other reveries,
the child's core turned inwards then outwards,
but he was never sure if the voice that called his name
had meant it to be this way.

BIBLIOGRAPHY

BIBLIOGRAPHY

The first novel I failed to write
was about two boys who made themselves
inscrutable, giggling at private jokes,
playing Kirk and Spock in turns.

The second novel I failed to write
started with a Dear John letter
and climaxed in a tower block flat
with a determined loneliness
I thought I could render heroic.

Then there was that novella
in which a broken-shouldered woman
with a plastic sheet
had only three wishes
and not one was granted her.

But the best novel I never wrote
began in the middle with a brazen revolution,
then leapt to the end, a holocaust of hopes,
before circling back to the beginning:
a shy child playing with a kaleidoscope,
re-organising the visible world.

ARDOURS OF ASCENT

The boy trudging up a green lane,
purple-lipped, out of breath, American,
is weighed down by a sodden rucksack
and the slack flatness of the hills.
The sky is grey. The land banal.
He doesn't know where to turn.
He keeps his alien tongue to himself.

As he climbs the green lane with no music in his ears
he's getting a lesson in powerlessness.
His boots pinch. His socks keep letting him down.

When the farmer stops to give him a lift,
he gives him a lift with memories of FDR and the New Deal.
Was it Cornwall or Shropshire?
Or Windermere, where Wordsworth died on the page
or the following summer, by the River Wye,
when the poem shouted itself back out of the ravine?

****

In the Himalayas, the narrow trail led upside,
through hamlets where red chillis dangled from trellises
and the charas was sticky and black.

****

Staring down, mesmerised
by your own feet consuming the pathway,
then lifting your gaze and taking in
the trail's steep curve,
the height still to be gained ...
these moments on the slow haul are bleak.
Unlike the cyclist, the only gears you can change
are in your mind.

****

The guide leapt from rock to rock,
showing how easy it was; but I couldn't dance his dance.
I need to stop at intervals, to catch my breath.
I need to look back, to assimilate
the distance that's been uncovered.

****

The monotony of switchbacks,
mitigated by dreams of upland meadows:
hovering, lushly grassed, pure of air, serene.
They make you think about cleaning up your act
until you realise it will never be enough.

****

Circling skywards towards a stone village
perched on an outcrop, showing blank walls
to the valley below,
brooding over injuries -
when I finally got there I found a sun-sealed square,
empty of life,
and a dark bar full of sullen faces.

****

At summer camp the others scooted ahead,
darting up the forest trail, flickering from light to shade
and back again,
leaving me behind, dragging my invisible anchor.
"Can't you see the anchor?" I wanted to cry,
but knew what I looked like, fighting tears, gasping for breath.
I looked like what I was: flabby, weak,
unfit for this mountainside and much else.

****

I was never more thirsty than when I reached the temple
balanced on a high peak under a gold and scarlet banner
only to find the tea stall closed.
I hadn't even come to pray.
I had no offering to make.
I watched a fat man on a litter being carried uphill
by four men half his size -
felt disgusted, envious and superior.

That's what its like climbing uphill -
it can test your patience,
twist your mind.

****

Some summits are let-downs:
loose scree, lesser clouds.
Others have been waiting just for you:
with a moss-cushioned seat, a sheltering tree,
and of course the big payback,
the reward for effort, the return on investment
so far beyond monetary value
it makes you want to laugh -
the view, the vastness
passing through the narrow retina
creating space inside the cramped mind,
unlocking the doorway to distance and scale.

****

There's the climb through jungle,
the climb over barren rock,
the climb up the mule track,
the climb up stairs, natural or artificial,
but the worst climb is the climb up asphalt roads
with their maddeningly dull gradient,
their predictability -
try as I might, I find in them no gift.

****

A few years ago,
somebody turned up the gravity dial,
tying boulders to my ankles
making each step an exercise
in the redistribution of weight,
the negotiation of a watershed.
Rising from the sofa is a resurrection.
Transferring my full weight to my own two feet
a summit surmounted.

In my condition it's all about staying grounded.
It's about understanding that all weight, all thrust,
is borrowed,
all leverage derived.

As I climb, I grind out the arguments.
I put my case. I cross-examine witnesses.
I wear them down with stubborn persistence.

****

I remember two elderly Englishwomen
climbing up a stony Tuscan lane
to visit the shrine of a saint in whom they did not believe.
Wary of all faiths, including their own,
armed with walking sticks
they made steady progress, filling the air with the low chirp
of conversation while I sweated
under the weight of my rucksack, tee-shirt and boots.

That night I camped alone in the forest,
sleeping not a wink as the sound of the saint -
martyred not for his faith but for his love,
martyred out of his love, with its own instruments -
moaned through the bat cries and jackal barks.
The end of that climb was not revelation
but fear and a passage through fear.

That's what it's like climbing uphill.
It's an equation - effort, elevation, field of vision -
a trigonometry in which the climber, not the summit
is the point of reference, the variable apex.

POETIC DICTION POETIC DICTION

This room steeped in twilight
is the only place where it's safe to speak
in the first person. Here in a darkness
as yet incomplete the word 'I'
can be uttered without terror.

There's space for the syllable
and its echo.

This room made of words
and the solace of words, of hesitation
and repetition, is breath
converted to being, sound protected
by silence, which is the shape of the room.

Neither child nor adult,
in this room I can be heard but not seen.

DO NOT BELIEVE THAT WE GROW

Do not believe that we grow.
We are born suddenly, out of a gesture,
a phrase, a cat cornered in the alleyway.

Do not believe that we grow.
It's all in the spurt, the clumsy revelation,
the lurch after stepping on a weak floorboard

as when I spotted a heaven within reach
like a loose ball down the leg-side,
swatted, struck air and toppled over.

It does not come naturally, like fruit from a tree.
It comes in gusts, in sheet lightening,
in slamming doors and broken windows

like a singer stepping forward
against a background of blaring violins
and hushing them with a sideways glance.

HOLD ON TO THAT DREAM (BEFORE IT HOLDS ON TO YOU)

My friends are cheerful, oblivious.
I can't remember them, not the way
they remember me. One has black hair
cut in a severe fringe that makes me wince.

We're packing up, clearing the apartment.
It's important we leave no trace.
Especially with the landlord on the premises.

What disturbs me most is how benign
he now appears. In silk dressing gown
with indecipherable monogram,
he's the friend of my friends.
The smile he wears is wry.

I turn away. I can't permit him
to see me seeing him. Even when I lived here
I always used the separate entrance,
buried in darkness at the rear.
I took care to make myself inaudible.
After I left, the apartment vanished.
It's strange now to be back, clearing away debris.

Somewhere outside, the queue for a flight
I need to board loops around itself.
Everyone shuffles with dull purpose.
It's a long haul flight to a distant homeland
which I've been meaning to catch for ages.
I've been meaning to make an exit, a return
but I'm still not ready to join the queue -
not while there's something forgotten,
not while some tell-tale scuff mark remains.

So I'm in the apartment avoiding the landlord,
averting my eyes, my heart thudding with animal fear
which I can't possibly share with my friends.
They're too straight, they dig the landlord
who asks with a smile, "Why won't Mike look at me?"
The pressure is mounting but I ferret away,
pretending not to know that he knows that I know
he's there and we share a past. How could I do otherwise?
The risks were too great.

The apartment has no windows
except for small, narrow ones through which
you can hope to see and not be seen.
It's sleeker than I remember
which makes me uneasy.
My notebook secrets exude a blurring dust.

All this is somewhere I don't want to be:
this is the main fact I have to keep hidden
from the multitude bobbing on the queue
and my friends combing the apartment.

Their appearance here remains a puzzle.
It takes a moment to grasp the implications.
How long have they been living here
on amiable terms with the landlord I'd studiously avoided?

I don't ask how they came to make themselves a home
in the home I'd never really lived in,
the home I abandoned years ago, without saying goodbye,
when I carried on a furtive existence from day to day.

These don't look like any friends I remember,
they don't look my type at all: they're too insouciant,
but they greet me as a friend
and prudently I don't dispute their claim.
I go along to get along, shielding my thoughts.
I betray no doubts, again and again,
especially not the doubts that put me here in the first place.

It's not a flat; it's an apartment, a division:
adjoining chambers encased within a larger structure,
anchored by that rear entrance buried in darkness.
The light inside is indirect, toneless
- an unpeacefully quiet light.
Or was it just me, just me in that light
that made it look that way,
me in that light amid my debris trying not to be seen?

Truth be told, I don't like my friends being here.
After all I'm not even sure I know them.
Of course I am careful to ensure they have no inkling,
especially no inkling of what it is that drives me
to hurry away the evidence, the drift.

Still, they've taken better care of the place than I did:
got the murk out of the light and the corners
now have clear-cut edges.

Peering behind a bookcase, it comes to me
how much I need to catch that long haul flight,
my only way back. But my passport is furry
as mouldy fruit and my tickets are in another pocket.
The queue folds around concrete pillars.
I have to get to the front but can't yet find the rear.
I have to loop back on myself.
My friends seem not to notice. Or are they being polite?

It's not a flat; it's an apart-ment
(apartness contained and cubified)
and behind its walls the landlord lives with his family.
I don't remember him being so debonair.
When I lived here he was a sullen presence,
now he's full of conversation,
which I find more ominous.

The people on the queue waiting to fly
have their tickets, passports and trolleys.
They line up not single file but two-three abreast
to disappear eventually into a dark doorway
of which I have glimpses while I scurry,
noiseless and desperate like a small rodent.

There's always more to tidy away,
another object, another embarrassment
I examine just long enough to remember
it's something I'd rather forget.

My friends are cheerful, meticulous;
the apartment shiny and bare
except for things that keep emerging from under cushions:
mostly paper, various grades and sizes, with writing ...

My friends are helpful, disturbing.

I keep a sharp eye out. I keep my mouth shut.
I've been here before in other dreams
and have never managed an escape.

STIFFENING IN AN EMBRACE

I stiffened in my father's embrace
and as soon as I could, pried myself loose.

It was an oceanic embrace,
an overflow, sweeping away
boundaries and swallowing up
counter-currents.

Close up, on the inside of the embrace,
I smelled sweat and sour breath.
I heard a heart pounding.

Yes, I stiffened in my father's embrace,
fearing I'd be lost in its amplitude.
I squirmed in my father's embrace
which was lumpy and thick like gravy,
sticky like syrup.

It was an ill-fitting embrace.
I got lost in the infinite chest
slipped through the prison-gate arms.

I was appalled by my own ingratitude.
I had failed to embrace the embrace
for which I was too small, too stiff,
too un-life-like. I fell through the cracks
and it was to be a long time before my father noticed
I was no longer there.

(Now in the mirror I see the features of the father whose embrace
made me squirm)

It was some kind of journey.
Trying to turn the cape but making no headway
I nearly gave up. Music from the fishermen's bar
supplied a tinny, trembly commentary
on the rage-warped, screw-tight, sunburnt figure
wrestling with his oars and his outboard in the empty bay.

The voices sliced through me, head to toe,
a clean cut with no ragged edges;
voices ringing off the cliff face
insistent most of all in their familiarity.

Even before then, I sat in traffic surrounded
by people who knew where they were going.

Hate is love's grubby companion,
it picks up love's broken pieces,
it has its own list of 40 things to do before you die,
but its shoals are poorly mapped...
I found myself driven far off course -
windless days, changeless scenery -
might as well have stayed at home.

The journey was a sequence of abstractions
given teeth and flesh to bury them in,
raining down like hard black flints.

Touching land was being touched by land
finding the touch painful
and deciding that enough was enough.

The voices remain insistent
long after they've ceased to be anything else.
They boom across the deck,
they couldn't care less where I'm going.
The only courage I could muster
was to catalogue the flaws in their logic,
their reliance on unexamined assumptions.

Impossible to make progress by day
I decamped by moonlight
when there was any. In the murk
I often stubbed my toe: the only relief
was effing and blinding.
Yet I dreaded the dawn like an insomniac
for whom the light breaking in the window
has the gavel ring of failure, with its sentence of more to come...

The journey brought me to the below-sea-level sea
where the air was heavy and the flies reigned.
Flies havocking eyebrows and earlobes.
Flies I imagined into existence on the shores of the below-sea-level sea
where dishevelled women pick tomatoes for export to their own country,
where it occurred to me that up till now I had not understood
the meaning of the word depression.

The car clatters at speed
over the rutted surface of a fiercely straight road -
even if I could bring myself to shout from the back seat
the driver would pay no heed.

No place to land that hasn't already been colonised,
deforested, erased by pre-emptive action.
The old trails the most disturbing,
with their fossilised remnants of an earlier life.

The watchtowers from which everyone looks small -
for years they made me climb them
arriving sweaty and ashamed of sweat.

Lonely Planet has no guide to these regions.
Even the archaeology is bitter stone,
just a pounding repetition of broken forms.

IN THE SHADOW OF THE BIG SELF

Misled from infancy, erroneous,
I set about building a new-better self
because the one I had been given seemed so paltry.

In the shadow of the self I built,
the self-contained self, the big self,
the little selves dwindled; many perished,
gone wherever withered selves go.

I'm thankful
for the ones that learned to thrive in the dark
despite my neglect.

ON THE THEME OF A HOMELAND

Prologue

On television the Australian novelist explains
why he doesn't like his country,
its selfishness and racism.

Unlike me, he's frank with himself
about what he dislikes and why.
He doesn't trim his views.

In his next book
he wants to address questions of success and failure,
he wants to know what we mean by success and failure,
he wants to pin down that difference.

The homeland: a remembrance

The homeland I remember
was glacial in colour, neutral in odour,
the beige pile vacuumed daily,
our debris removed before we could notice it.
It was the time of the Cold War and the domino theory,
the heyday of utilitarian design.

Formica surfaces with sticky patches
chocolate cakes and lamb chops
everywhere cries for attention

The homeland I remember
was chaotic, like the stock exchange,
under-bidding and over-selling,
clamorous, imperious:
feed me, tuck me in, read me a story,
tickle my back, drop me off, pick me up,
buy me a toy, a book, a pez dispenser,
stop him / her doing this / that.
Voices bouncing off the ceiling
crashing into the dinner table,
teasing, goading, baiting, prodding....
we looked for a reaction
but every time it was a chain reaction.

Chaotic, like a playground melee.
Too many broadcasters crowding on the same waveband;
what couldn't be assimilated littered the kitchen floor.

Breakfast was coldly tactile
egg-smeared cheeks
jam on the butter knife
the sourness of orange juice in toothpaste mouths
cranky moods clattering against each other like dishes

We tried too hard too much of the time,
presenting symptoms - jaw aches,
curling toes, rashes of varying shades.
Some of us developed allergies to strange situations,
others reacted only to the familiar.

It was raucous. The opposite of music.
In the din my voice sounded shrill and strange.
Our laughter when it came was hysterical.

It was crowded.
At the dinner table my elbows poked out too far.
The house was so big we kept bumping into each other.
Contact was hard: skull on skull, knee on knee,
ego on ego. We memorised pain thresholds.
We were prepped to seize on a grievance -
any hint that we were not getting our fair share
or that others were getting more than theirs.
We waited for a slip-up, an exposure,
our own or somebody else's.

It was cold, like the uncreated pointless universe
bodies spinning in an empty medium
with nothing to cushion them:
momentum was all, angles of deflection
reactions and rebounds.
Alliances were impermanent.

Estrangement ruled the house.
The sadness brimmed over but no one felt it.
(No one was allowed to feel it).

Everything was over-illuminated.
I searched the house for shadows.

My job

The division of personalities
like the division of labour under capitalism
was arbitrary and oppressive.

My job was leader of the pack.
Our barking was outrageous.
How was it the neighbours never complained?

Praise was a hammer.
They laid you on an anvil
and beat out the asymmetries.

You could only eat too little or too much.
The happy medium
was always held against us.

To hear myself think
I had to turn up the volume of my thoughts,
clear a circle and hunker down inside it.

Hiding places

Once I ran away
into the dark heart of the suburban garden
where I huddled behind the rhododendron
waiting to be missed and discovered.

After a while I gave up and struck camp.
My escapade had passed unnoticed.
I was back in the fold as if nothing had happened
and I wanted something to happen,
for years I wanted something to happen
but it seemed to be happening somewhere else.

In the garage I built a model of the solar system.
In the garage where the light came from outside,
a rectangle of brightness from the driveway,
I devoured baseball statistics like pornography.

In this architecture, the interiors
had no interior. The sources,
heat, light, water,
were hidden out of sight.
Too neat! Too neat! I cried
and stayed up late, watching
movies interrupted by adverts.

It was so unbearably banal that to give it substance
I stole other people's memories
and stuffed my head with other people's myths.
At 13 I took the bus to the nearest shopping centre
to ride the escalators with a friend.

At 14 I took the train to Greenwich Village
to sit in cafe darkness inhaling smoke
and getting hit over the head by the same three chords.

There's nothing I want to recapture from this past
except the hiding places.

Nostalgia

Nostalgia? For a place without place?
No one exiled or banished me.
The route home has always been open.

When I think of my homeland
it 's not jasmine I smell
but turkey TV dinners and air freshener.

The surprise of these memories is like
reaching inside and touching ice
in the hot depths of your own bowels.

After words

I heard a Palestinian poet say
the homeland is not an inheritance.
It's what you make of what you find
in the wasteheaps of history and your own heart.
It's not where you come from
but where you're going to.
It's a place of arrival and rest.

I heard a child being promised
the distance travelled from the homeland
is a second homeland
which like a second sun
disperses the shadows cast by the first,
doubling the highlights,
lighting up the underside,
painting the world with a gentler brush.

ONLY IF I COULD WALK

Seeing I was so far gone -
a friend said women liked that
sleepless, haunted look -
I slipped on boots and maps,
covered my ears,
scoured my ipod for a theme tune...

Only if I could walk
not great distances but far enough
to lose one way and make another.

I remembered the thin woollen shawl
spread flat on concrete
that was a good place to spend the night,
accompanied by moth-mottled lights
and the sweet fatigue of an army of sleepers.

But every thing is given to me backwards,
it's slipped to me in a crowded market,
unwrapped and unlabelled.

Seeing I was so far gone -
watching television serials in reverse order
- I took steps to jettison debris,
however gilded or deliciously wasted,
memory-trimmed but not really mine.

Only I wanted to imagine
images stamped with a mark
incised and proud, a token
of their maker's mind.

Only I wanted that dream where everything is recuperated
where the indignant cries of the gods are ignored
and the bass line is strong.

I wanted the beach, the black sea weed beach in Maine
I wanted the beach, the black tar beach in Bombay
and people drinking tea under dusty awnings
looking up briefly as I pass.

This is my blue-tinted retreat
with a selection of suns to suit every mood
- seeing I was so far gone.

YOU HEART

YOU HEART

How easily seduced, you heart,
you throbbing muscle of need,
you greedy gobbler -
one whiff of paradise and you're on the next plane out.

Always hungering,
with your childishness
and adult language,
your persistent absenteeism.

You never knew how to haggle -
letting yourself get snapped up, again and again,
at bargain prices,
selling your loyalties cheap.

You never thought what you were getting me into.
You never thought of the wear and tear.
Curfew breaker
how many lies did I tell on your behalf?

Utopian desperado,
clinging to hypotheses,
seizing on the slightest evidence,
shrinking at the incompassionate touch.

Cruelty
caught you unprepared.
Easily snared, casually released,
you never toughened up.

Hurt pump,
pawing at the future,
hanging on to early investments
your archives in perpetual disarray...

For years I fed you scraps, I know,
let you walk abroad only after midnight.
Inveterate yearner,
I was the inconstant one, not you.

Off-stage thunderer, quaking
the auditorium, shivering the audience,
hinter, hesitator,
help me now.

Tell me where the river can be found
to slake your enormous thirst,
the river of many waters,
where you can break yourself open and bleed.

I cannot read you, never could.
Speak plainly now,
choose the music,
steer me into open spaces.

THE BOOK OF LIZ

THE WAIT WILL NOT BE LONG

I hear the rustle of the bicycle returning to its shed,
the thrust and clunk of lock and bolt.

Indoors and all at once, the weather shifts,
like an orchestra changing key.

I hear carpet-thumps, muffled bumps,
and a sigh.

I hear the winter coat dropped to the floor
and a hurried rush for the loo.

She brings in warmth from the cold outside,
she melts the ice within.

She's invisible but near: my protector, my mediator
- my central heating.

RECURRING PROTAGONIST

She's my recurring protagonist, my lady detective,
whose genteel eccentricities mask fire and steel.
She chirps in the garden but her justice is swift.

She's my lady detective in a dark suit,
eating on the run, mobile to ear,
an innocent entrapping the corrupt, step by step.

She puzzles over lists, logs details for later reference.
She reads books about forgotten Cabinet members
and solves cases while pretending not to.
She's vivacious, self-effacing, fatally underestimated.

With an unspoiled mind she unravels
the mystery of the immigrant's assassin,
uncovers the police cabal in the masonic lodge,
puts the agent provocateur in the dock.

She's unarmed, knows no martial art, takes up little space.
She's vulnerable, which readers like.
She's resilient, which they like even more.

Crimes of money, passion, stupidity,
she's always unprejudiced.
Even when she makes witnesses cry
they cry on her shoulder.

She peppers her discourse with apologies.
She's embarrassed by her laugh.
But observation, she has learned, is a cold tool:
that's how she caught the sub-prime trader in his own net.

Beneath the distracted surface, the gullible dimples,
wheels turn within wheels, small cogs
govern great chains of logic.
She drinks her coffee black and by the hour.

She's prone to the occasional panic -
flummox shows on her face – but always
she regathers, refocusses. She narrows the beam
along the track of the probable, however improbable.

Her movements are lateral. She takes the long way around
to arrive at exactly the right spot.
When she unmasked the gang rapists at the High Table
her elfish face looked daintily pained.

She's a lady detective with a human touch,
saddened when she has to send someone to jail.
All in all, she'd rather watch a DVD with her boyfriend,
who is a figure representing the mundane, like furniture.

TOGETHER ALONE HER ALONE

Finally we've seen off the guests
and are together alone.
The house is ours,
a zone of intimacy, binding but elastic.
We carry it with us from room to room.
Nothing needs to be said so whatever is said
is light, free, airy – feathers in the air around us
pillowing our lazy dance
but never settling on the carpets or cushions.

In the beginning we were illicit,
each of us tied to a third party.
(No one was supposed to get hurt.)
We were unofficial lovers.

Our initiation to each other was furtive,
a lift after a meeting, a meeting of eyes,
an accumulation of confidences,
things shielded from public view
even before our conference week rendez-vous
in a bare hotel room with a view of grey sea.

Our foundations were laid in secret,
their solidity in shared indiscretion,
now as then.

Together alone, we inhabit
this zone of intimacy where there's
no bureaucracy, no observers,
no sanction. Now as then
our love is strictly unofficial.

NO LIZ BUT LIZ

For a long time I studied you in your sleep.
I watched phosphorous stick figures
dance on your forehead, then dissolve.

You snuggle down. In the folds of the duvet,
you're a protected species: I will permit no one
to wrench you from this habitat,
this sleep of the just.
I take my guard, book in hand, and mumble
a vow heard once in a movie.

Your skin is lit from within,
like olive oil, warm and scented,
a golden aura showing through a pink-green flush.
Sometimes I take notes:
that soft nasal gasp is your sleep renewing itself.
You are my field of research,
a discipline with all the trappings,
and I am Chair of the Department.

When you look up from under dark startled arches
and for a moment show me eyes like troubled pools ...
whatever the problem, I want
to grab and smother it.
I want to secret it away and stamp it out.

You are not a god far off.
You are a sister and a friend, near at hand
like a pocket or a book of poems.
Nothing distinguishes your presence or your absence
like your presence or your absence
unless it's the white streak in your dark fringe
or the dark fringe dragged back from eyes
rich as deep-stained mahogany.

I will not worship false idols, as others do.
There is no Liz but Liz.
You dispense with wigs and gowns.
You annul the old stale laws
which is why in many societies
they divide time on earth into the eras
before and after your coming,
a coming foretold - yes, it was written
in such and such a month and year
Liz would come and Mike
would never be the same.

'Blasphemer!' you purr at me,
indulging my extravagance even in your sleep.

When it comes to me you take a holistic approach -
refraining from amputations, surgical probes,
blood letting in moderation only, and even then
more for the placebo effect than anything else.

There is no Liz but Liz.
She soothes the heretic's ragged temper.
She is my shepherd.
She will not forsake me.
She maketh me to lie down in front of the TV.
And I will have no Liz but Liz.

For a long time I studied you in your sleep.
I watched phosphorous stick figures
dance on your forehead, then dissolve.

NIGHT AFTER NIGHT

When I creep into our bed late at night
and wake you with the gentlest touch I can manage,
even before your eyes have opened
you're pleased; pleased that it is me,
pleased that night after night it is always me.

Way back a thunder-clap.
You sitting across a table at a fund-raising social,
the table cluttered with glasses and me
wanting to touch you. You
speaking in an earnest I recognised.
I thought: she has the difference
my difference has been looking for.

I wish I could climb into your dreams and plant there
messages of love that would activate in your sleep.
Night after night I'd murmur my tender cliches,
I'd renew my superfluous vows.

When I become a ghost, I promise
not to haunt the house.
But summon me any time
and I'll be there at speed, by your side,
bearing my ghostly affirmations.

WE'LL HANG PICTURES TOGETHER

Let's climb the ladder to look at the stars
before the cloud creeps in from the sea.
Let's taste the silence, the brittle night air,
the tonic of stillness, darkness and space.

Tomorrow we'll hang pictures together
without a spirit level, stepping back
and peering, first one, then the other
asking who or what is really tilted.

We'll play each other like instruments,
teach each other like students.
We'll be each other's sun-and-moon,
source and reflection.

Let's climb the ladder to look at the stars,
but only for a moment: waiting downstairs
in a curtained room is our common bed
with its sweet rites and sustainable warmth.

THE VASE ON THE MANTELPIECE

Light from the window falls on the vase on the mantelpiece,
the vase with two handles and one swollen belly.
Three shades of blue, a milky white and a child's yellow
tremble in the depths of its glaze.
The floral pattern is Persian.
The stout neck is strapped in silver bands, like the bride
it was made for, and like the wedding it celebrates
the vase is cheerful, homely and lopsided.
Empty of water or oil or grain, it contains nothing but itself.
Empty of water or oil or grain, it's still our libation -
the vase of our marriage, in the high wastes of north London,
on the far side of custom and law.

ND PERSON

You are always you, the second person singular.
Even when you're out of earshot,
even when you've left orbit,
you remain the second person,
the ever-present addressee,
the informal you, the intimate you,
the listening and answering you.

Threatened by meaning, frightened by depth,
the undeceived march in rank.
If I linger behind or cross to the other side,
I know your hand is in mine.

The weekend of the empty skies
when distance returned to its natural dimensions
when the future ground to a halt but nothing changed
I watched you busy in the garden
where emulating Blake in Lambeth, we keep
a fig tree, olive and vine.
(On sunlit days they're happy.)
Your struggle with the long forking branches
was Chaplinesque.

Like desert vegetation, my green heart
breaks through crusted sand
to bask in your light;
my roots reach for your rain.

How is it that you're not an intruder?
How is it that your flesh doesn't vanish at my touch?
This is the witch-craft they should have burned you for,
the daily miracle of Liz in the second person singular.

Meanwhile in the first person plural,
we're blessed with a late nakedness,
one that matures long after we've taken off our clothes.

I will survive as a sphere beyond a final sphere
waiting patiently for news of those I left behind.
The form will be strange but the content familiar.

I will wait especially for news that mentions you,
news of your interventions and escapades.
My sphere will turn gold when you are gold,
grey when you are lost in thought,
spring-green when, after winter indoors,
your face opens again to light and warmth.

I will wait lonely as that sphere
rolling through its silent heaven,
casting no shadow, reflecting no light,
but I will have time to read the book we wrote together
with is bittersweet twists and deep unintentional structure:
the long boom of love.

I will survive as a sphere beyond a final sphere
in an orbit of my own,
knowing that your news will search me out.
I will await the outcome of your every match.
I will never bet against you.

THE DIAMOND'S ROLE

LIKE A PALM TREE

Morning in the newspaper, cardamom in the coffee
- it all savours of an aftermath
cool as lime, a moment with wind in its sails.

The breeze turns in a slow arc, outwitting the captain.
The clouds shrink before a blue distance.
Everything lies only a giant step away.

An aftermath is always of a fore-moment -
a clash of heads, a misused verb - where the present
shades us from the past, like a palm tree.

OPENING PAIR OPENING PAIR

One of us drops anchor
while the other gets off to a flyer.
It's not because one's more impetuous
or cautious than the other.
The assault, like the defence, is calculated.
We play the same percentages
to different rhythms, following
our own sequence
of stressed and unstressed beats,
each of us fashioning
our own departure from the norm.
After the crescendo, the rest,
after the rest, the crescendo.
One of us foil for the other, as it should be.

Personality will out.
We perform in our styles
because that is our function.
We never get in each other's way.
We perform who we are
because that is what the situation demands -
but at a pinch we can swap roles,
one coming out from the shadow of the other.

THE THICK GREY SOUND OF THIN BLUE RAIN

The shelter from the rain
is under red arcades lined with coffee houses.

The downpour hisses like a furtive voyeur.
The droplets bounce off the black road,
the plaited streams snake down the drains.
Up close but safe from the torrent,
dry in a deluge: it has the feel of luxury.

The waiting for the rain to cease
becomes a precious ellipsis.
We get a taste for the waiting,
for the moment of suspension,
sipping a hot drink under the red arcade,
keeping the damp at bay like a yapping pet.

We get a taste for the serendipity,
the incidental completeness
in the shelter humming with idle thoughts,
hemmed in and cuddled, comforted
by the the thick grey sound of thin blue rain
hurtling from above like a forest of sharpened pencils.

STOKE NEWINGTON *BULERIAS*

See how the bar-light spreads into the streets,
how the streets embrace it in candid arms?

The pavement glistens with a thin wash of beer,
the hopsy air kicks back, adrenalin-like.

We're all a little boozed up, a little off-centre
our heads floating weightlessly in night air.

Church Street and High Street in a pas de deux
quick-stepping on each others' tender feet.

It's a dance of temporary marriages,
a dance of stumbles and knee-clacking,

juggling second thoughts, impurities,
taking turns, showing off with wobbly twirls.

The dance is raucous with giddy highs
and gritty lows, but the compas is sure.

The compas is ebullient, swelling,
sotto voce. It crackles like a fire.

The minutes climb and linger like hours.
The hours tumble and blaze like seconds.

They sweep us off our feet, hold us upright.
They stretch us out, bunch us together.

My head is loco from the all the suspense.
Tonight I'll speak to a listening moon.

Tonight I'll throw stones at roving dumpsters
and if they hit anyone I'm sorry.

ACCEPTING AN OFFERING

A woman with a blue accent
on a morning of cloud and sun
hailed me from a distance.

I couldn't make out the words
but I heard the voice - rounded,
rolling, like a path over small hills.

Her stride was nonchalant.
A smile joined her mouth and eyes.
She advanced

across spaces that opened and closed
before and behind her
with the whisper of bead curtains.

I knew her birthright: I knew
the ease, the mobility that meant
the distance between us would remain.

Yet her advice was benign,
her irony mild and her accent blue.
There was no coyness in it.

Her syllables never broke ranks
or cut anyone short.
Her sentences were long-tempered.

On a morning of sun and cloud,
she made her offering from a distance
and I thought I might as well accept it.

WINTERING WINTERING

Wintering calls for chicanery. High walls,
right angles, deflections. Running battles,
coded messages, hide-and-seek.
Deep recesses, the rigour of rumour,
the sly wisdom of the upturned collar.
It's an exercise in discretion.

(I am snow covered
I bristle with pine
I play with the fading light like a football
My arms are spread wide
I surf the gale from the north)

Wintering involves indoors. Shadows
and the protection of shadows,
firelight, steam-blurred glass,
sideways ritual: coming in from the cold,
drying out and warming up. Wintering
is improvising an interior.

(My arms are spread wide
I surf the gale from the north
I am snow covered
I bristle with pine
I play with the fading light like a football)

My friend had good reasons for making his pain a private affair.
Alone in a small room it could be brought down to size.
Alone in a small room it was an interlocutor he could contend with.

Here he could negotiate with it face-to-face.
His position was that he would endure the cramp in his limbs
if the ache in his heart was eased - or was it the other way around?
His strategy was to concede nearly everything.
But his hand was weak and his clumsy opponent
showed unanticipated finesse.

Over a drink in the pub, submerged in a medium
of anonymous noise,
I glimpsed him squaring off with his pain.
I overheard the sharp, accusatory dialogue.
I knew it would be wrong to intrude.

My friend had good reasons for making his pain a private affair,
a secret rendezvous on the stage of an empty theatre.

With its intimacy, its invasiveness,
their intercourse teetered on the brink of the obscene.
He couldn't endure playing it out in front of an audience,
no matter how select.

In private he could measure the intervals
between notes, each note
combining duration, pitch and something else -
a way of sliding into and out of itself,
a special relationship with silence.
Each note an impress on a nerve, a tender spot
sounded out like a potential informer.

He measured the intervals,
the space that separated one hurt from another,
the time that joined them in a single pain,
the pain that could only be a private affair -
safe from observation,
contained in a small room with soft curtains,
contained in a small room locked from the inside.

It was a pain impossible to publish without making the headlines
either too big or too small.

RESPITE

Trying to get away from the feeling
that I can't get away from them,
that they're everywhere, perched on lamp posts,
peeking through branches, spying
from chimney grates and alarm systems...
I leave work to sit alone at a stranger's grave,
the letters incised with tapering serifs
on close-grained weather-worn stone.

Today I'm not concerned with dates or names.
I don't want to be another inquisitor.
I'm only concerned
with the beech trees arching overhead
and the commonality of the graveyard.
I want to erase the inscriptions
so that no life can be labelled.
I want leaves to settle over the graves
in a blanket of anonymity -
so that we intruders learn to seek
from the company of the dead
only their blithe silence,
their lesson in inequality.

LAMENT

Once I had a father
but I misplaced him
where the River Lea flows into the Cauveri
and the gods are bulbous, frisky and stout.

Once I had a teacher
who left me on a mountain-side
rapt by a view of peach-tinted clouds
playing at marriage and divorce.

Once I had a lover -
I abandoned her in a small town
equipped with a giant multiplex,
a life of no subtitles and jittery camerawork.

Once I had two friends,
they disappeared with their instruments
above the tree-line, where the snow
is forked with bird-tracks.

REUNION (CHENNAI, 2010)

Being with you again reminds me of my lost naivete
and how little I miss it.

The charm of our first meeting was its serendipity.
The two of us, mutually unaware,
coming face to face only because my passport had been stolen.

Your manners were stilted, slowed by ceremony and humidity.
My gorging curiosity was hidden, poorly, behind sunburn.

You must remember how politeness turned to familiarity
amid leg-glances and quarter-tones? The melisma
was thrilling. The funerary histrionics,
miasmic ditches, gargantuan hoardings -
all were paths to your ample, indifferent heart.

I cherished those anecdotes of quainter times,
tales of your mentors and, later, your tormentors.
Serpentine tales of allegiance and betrayal,
long innings played with a dead bat.

We've changed, but not in tandem. Your scent
of cardamom and diesel has a burnt-offering quality.
You're girdled in a superstructure of cement.
Your deco parapets and racy bungalows
are streaked and ravaged;
their gardens wilt in the fumes.

As I've grown slower you've grown faster.
The stately pace, the roomy avenues are gone.
The prizes you offer have multiplied to no purpose - "growth"'s
relics litter the street's edge where scavengers, greedy,
narrow chested, puzzle their uses.

Still, there's the sour taste of our breakfasts together,
the young fermentation welcoming us to a day
of discounted treasures and cheerful haggling.

THE SUN SPRAWLING IN THE STREET

Today's light hovers in narrow windows.
Their modesty is a sign of the city
before plate-glass gaped and dwindled us.
A brickwork smell freshens the air.
Buses are at peace with pedestrians.

A woman lifts her face to the sun
whose warmth falls over her like a shawl.
The sun lies down on the pavement
and rises up a new being, its good mood
banishing petulant shadows.

In the green square lit up with fresh growth
and pale roses, blown men congregate,
nurse their cans and find much to discuss.
On this day, theirs is not a sad fate
(though sadness lurks in pools at their feet).

The shops are over-run by school uniforms,
loud with the medley of trivia and taunt.
Each child sports a tilted halo, trashy,
glorious, if somewhat awry, like the imps
who wear them, exuberant and brooding.

The blown men in the green square ignore
the children bellowing in shops who fail
to notice the woman caressed by the sun
which sprawls in the street like a lazy cat
indiscriminate in its affections.

THE OBVIOUS

Wearing nothing out of the ordinary,
the obvious sits down beside me.
Her presence is strangely soothing;
I feel no need to impress or interrogate her
though I know I'm not her natural associate
because it bothers me
that I can't think of anything to say to her
that isn't obvious.

Her manner is reassuring
as if she knows I'm a novice
to be introduced slowly to her ways;
her indifference to all but the self-evident
shocks me at first. She's exactly
what I had given up expecting
but I notice that when she sits beside me
the light shifts, as if relieved of purpose,
and people walk more easily.

I fall silent but it's OK
because there's no mystery in the silence,
it's all obvious, as is the fact
that this will be a fleeting visit
and in future I'll know her mainly by her absence.

THIS MORNING'S SURPRISE

THIS MORNING'S SURPRISE

This morning's surprise is how much I'll miss rail travel.
The green fields looming up and falling behind,
the milky tea wobbling in a plastic cup,
the engine's steady vibration.

This afternoon's surprise is how many shades of red there are,
each one sitting in a room of its own, dense in meditation.
Each one a field of conflict, a medium of conciliation.

This evening's surprise is not that the novel ends
in a desultory return to the working week -
loose ends trimmed and tucked out of sight -
but the ferocity of my recoil
at the author's glib contrivance.

Midnight's surprise is Lorca's moon floating over Hackney
full-faced, round-eyed and speaking Spanish.

THE DIAMOND'S ROLE

Open the box to find the box within the box
but don't rush it.
Inside there's a couplet from a ghazal
sarcastic as an almond cracked between the teeth.
(The victim thanks God he went unnamed.)

But there are other thumbnails.
Profiles cached and dispersed. Time saved
in slender test tubes with rubber stoppers.
Inside every mechanism is a mystery,
a concatenation of symbols.

The stone blocking our path
was rolled in our way long before we were born.
It's the size of a house and smells of camomile.
On its jaw is a day's growth of grey-green stubble.
This was back then, when there were holidays
for children who had never watched TV.
If you stayed too long near the stone, it was said,
you'd become the stone.

Like creases, the nervous twitches can be ironed out.
Carpet-like, they can be beaten from a balcony.
Something must play the diamond's role:
incisive, translucent, correct.

AFTER THE BATTLE

Two armies circled each other in the forest.
Combat was attritional, resolved only by a truce
signed in a distant city. After which soldiers
drifted from the front, headed west, turned free lance.

We all need a break
from our roles in long running TV series,
from our duties as ambassadors, however informal.

We met where the canal bends like an elbow
to smoke a joint and plan our campaign.
I wandered off on my own under the big chestnuts
certain there was a heaven within reach.

After the battle
we were honoured for our role in seeing off the coup.
As our names were read out on the radio
lights flashed from a tower block,
lights in the night for each of us.
I waited my turn for applause. I waited my turn to speak.
Notes for the speech were in my pocket.

We all need a break
from our roles in long running TV series,
from our duties as ambassadors, however informal.

Even the once great moon is reduced to a sliver.
In Herschel's day it was populous,
fortified and urbanised,
but it must've stared down on too many human nights
and lost its nerve.

All around us a multitude of pasts,
our own and others',
humming like powerlines in the dark.

All around us, the dead - nation-states,
musical genres, strivers and shirkers -
diffused through the atmosphere
in nearly weightless particles.

All around us, a history not of our making.
All around us, a breath saturated with loss.
All around us, but out of reach,
loves that perished, affections that withered.

All around us, the day of the future,
its lungs braced with fresh air,
its eyes devouring the horizon,
its speech sparkling with metaphors,
its song so strong it never rises above a whisper.

All around us, the day of the strong songs.
All around us, a future like a cloud of unknowing.
All around us, the hour of liberation
ringing out from telephone masts
piercing the news cycle.

I can't remember where I heard the rumour
but it's all around us, latent, invisible,
under our feet, over our heads,
within our grasp.

Acknowledgements

Aditya Sarkar read and re-read nearly all of these poems in various stages of composition. His comments and insight have made all the difference. Steve Faulkner, comrade-poet, listened with an acute ear and open heart, commented and encouraged. Lachlan Stuart offered fresh perspectives and welcome reassurance. Rab MacWilliam, editor, publisher and Stoke Newington chronicler, is responsible for turning the manuscript into a book; his advice and support has been invaluable.

About Clissold Books

Clissold Books is an independent and innovative publisher based in Stoke Newington, the historically dissident heartland of North London.

We publish across a variety of areas, including music, local history, poetry, sport, philosophy, current affairs and popular culture generally. Whatever their subject matter, our books are written by accomplished and highly regarded authors, and are accessible, informative and radical in their own ways. We pride ourselves on ensuring that they are also thought provoking and entertaining.

Visit our website and discover more about us.

www.clissoldbooks.com

clissold**books**